I Do Romance Vows Husband & Wife Love Forgiveness
PoetryRing
Of
Marriage
II
Phyllis E. Griffin
I0836452

HerLife HerWrite Publishing Co. LLC
ISBN: 978-1-7373740-4-6

Dear Heavenly Father,

I give you glory for your inspiration to write your book. I pray that you will use these words to bless marriages and to bless & encourage those who desire to be married in Jesus (Yeshua)'s name.

Amen.

Table of Content

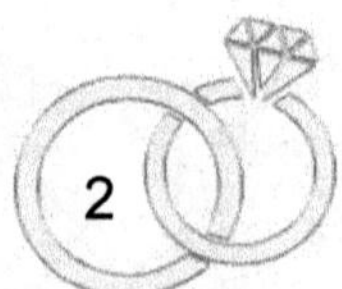

Commitment

Commitment is love that has stick and stay
It is love that will be there for many days

Commitment is love that will persevere
It is love that is reverent and has godly fear

Commitment is love that last through life's storms
It is love that is accepting and is truly warm

Commitment is love that will go through the ups and downs
It is love that will love you, even when you wear a frown

Commitment is love when the money gets low
It is love that makes you stay rather than go

Commitment is swallowing your pride and telling God, yes
It is love that is determined to do your very best

Commitment is staying when times get really, really hard
It is love that remains even when you're dealt some
difficult cards

Commitment is sometimes suffering the wrong
It is love that will lead you to God's merciful throne

Commitment is taking care of each other in sickness and in
health
It is love that is devoted and true beyond financial wealth

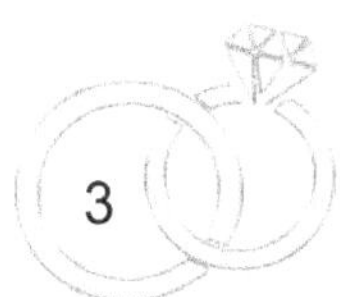

Commitment is doing what you need to do, being where you need to be
It is love that knows your spouse and family are depending on thee

Commitment, Commitment is not to be taken lightly
For we know that God will respond to us precisely

The Sanctity of Marriage

Marriage is a union that should not be entered into irresponsibly
God is its author, and he expects each spouse to behave uprightly

The sanctity of marriage is not old fogey neither is it a fable
The God who ordained and called it forth, Honey, He is able!

Marriage is a journey of two lives together, having one united vision
It takes operating in understanding and compromise, to remedy all kinds of division

The things that happen between a husband and his wife
Are written down in God's book, throughout eternal life

He is the godly and holy witness between the two
He is their stick and stay power, their supernatural glue

He called them together to do and fulfill his plan
He is their defense against the wiles of satan and woes of man

Marriage is still holy in the sight of God, our Father
It is close and dear to his heart, so be careful not to bother

Marriage came out of the very mind and heart of God
He created it, so to him it's not impossible or odd

God called a man to be a man, a woman to be a woman
They are to rejoice in the things that they have in common

Both spouses should be willing to stand their ground
God expects them to cultivate their relationship and keep it sound!

Break the Curse of Divorce with the Blood

You don't have to labor under the curse or fear of divorce
Mind you, you will have to deal with the spirit or influence of it, of course

You don't have to labor under the fear of what happened to your mother or father
Remember that the Almighty God is your redeemer and your author

You don't have to believe that what happened to others has to happen to you
You must know and believe that God's living word is infallible and true

You don't have to treat your spouse wrongly because of the fear of what might happen
Instead, allow your relationship to be filled with love, grace, and a lot of joy-filled laughing

Yes, divorce happens and no one should feel condemned or demeaned
Know that God is right there with you, He is right there on the scene

He knows everything you've gone through and loves you just the same
He's not assigning blame to you because of his love, the blood of Jesus (Yeshua), and his Holy Name

The blood of Jesus (Yeshua) is victory over all strife and woes
It will cause the enemy to take up his mess and have a case of 'the goes'

The blood of Jesus will conquer every curse and every bad thing
Learn to speak its power and unto the Lord God, break out and sing

Learn to declare the blood of Jesus over your family and marriage
Know that you've been given authority and in it, you can take advantage

Break the curse, Break the curse of divorce and generational blunders
Break the curse through the blood of Jesus (Yeshua), Break it in sunder!

Help create a new generation and a sound path for marital relationships
Through his blood, you can help establish long-lasting, united partnerships

Believe that you can be the one, that can break destructive generational molds
Yes, you can do it if you declare the power of the blood firmly and bold!

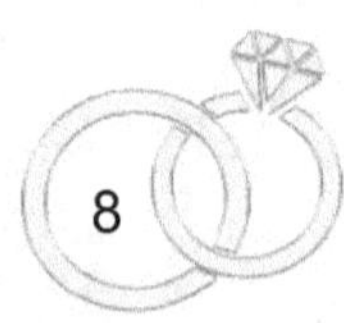

Don’t get stuck by being afraid of a marital commitment, or fearing a divorce
Believe and Declare the conquering blood of Jesus (Yeshua).
Do it with firmness and with godly force!

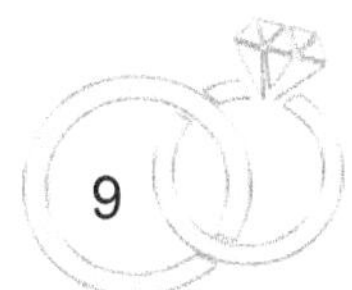

Why are You Picking a Fight?

Why are you picking a fight?
Constantly fussing and arguing, you know it's not right.

Bringing up old stuff, dead stuff, and stuff that don't make any sense
If I had the energy, I would just run and jump over the fence.

You make it difficult to stay with you
with all the fussing and griping you do.

However, I look pass it and try hard to see the good
Please remember you're confessing God, so stop acting like you're in the hood.

Your words at times are grievous, filled with bitter pain
They cast a weight on my spirit and cause mental strain.

Why can't we live in peace together, day in and day out?
Why must you raise your voice, project it, and then... you have to shout?

I try my best to please you, show you my devoted love
However, you refuse to acknowledge me and the One up above.

The bible says that a soft answer, it turns away wrath
Do you understand how desperately we need to walk down this very path?

If I've done something wrong, please just let me know
Because I really and truly want our relationship to grow.

If you're holding unforgiveness toward me because of the past
Please...please, let it go so our relationship can last.

You fuss, fuss, fuss, I guess to hear yourself talk
You need to rethink the situation or I may have to walk.

The continual fussing and griping is getting on my last nerve
Will you take a chill pill, and remember who we serve?

So please... stop all this fussing and arguing, I tell you once more
If you can't do that, can you please... go in the room, and shut the doggone door?

Stop Playing the Dozens

Stop playing the dozens with one another
You should respect the mother of each other

Stop putting down the mother of your mate
You don't know her story that is written on heaven's slate

Stop pitting the daughter against the one that bore her
Be respectful and kind with your words, please Sir

Stop pitting the son against the one that brought him into this world
If you knew her story, it might make your head spin or swirl

Stop all of this, "Your Momma that and your Momma this"
Remember, it was the love of a mother that gave you your first kiss

Stop bringing up your spouse's mother's mistakes of the past
If you continue to do so, your marriage probably won't last

Stop all of this, "Your Momma ain't this and your Momma ain't that"
Your lack of respect and regard for a mother shows where you're really at

You're at a place of utter disrespect, polluted with willful, ugly pride

My brother, my sister, you're headed for a very destructive and painful ride

If you can't say anything good to her mother or about her, please close your mouth
Because if you persist with this, your relationship just might go south

Learn to respect the mother of your mate, do it from the heart
For the person who chooses to do this, the Lord Himself, will regard

Agree to Disagree

We may not see everything eye to eye
But does our love and relationship have to die?

We may not agree on every single, solitary point
But can we trust our hearts to God, that he will anoint?

Anoint with tenderness, forgiveness, and divine understanding
Because we do know, the marriage is not about demanding or commanding?

We may see things from different views or perspectives
But can we work together to make our marriage effective?

We may not always agree with each other's opinions
But can we humble ourselves under God's divine dominion?

We may sometimes struggle to defer to one another
But can we remember our first days together when our hearts did flutter?

We may quarrel sometimes, have our say, or even speak our piece
But can we please keep our marital business out of the streets?

We must agree to disagree without being bitter and cold

Shouldn’t we respond this way in order to protect our
marital soul?

We must agree to disagree when conversations become
heated and intense
Shouldn’t we act mature, respectful, and do the things
which make godly sense?

We must agree to disagree instead of being overcome with
old, stupid pride
Shouldn’t we exchange pride for humility, instead of,
letting it take over and divide?

Agreeing to disagree helps us to keep walking side by side
and hand in hand
Isn't it better to build our lives on this principle, rather than
on stinking, sinking sand?

Love is a Two-Way Street

As we walk down this street called Love
We should be getting our directions from God above

We realize this street flows in both directions
Therefore, we both should show loving affection

Love is a two-way street where serving should be a mutual agreement
Each spouse doing for each other, exercising love and equal treatment

Love is a two-way street where each spouse shares in the daily load
Humbly, tenderly doing their part, ensuring the relationship doesn't implode!

Love is a two-way street where forgiveness should flow from heart to heart
If it is practiced often, the enemy won't be able to set us apart

Love is a two-way street where submission should be practiced spouse to spouse
If it is observed, peace and understanding will dwell and remain in the house

Love is a two-way street where healthy and honest communication should flow

It is this kind of communication that helps the marriage to
flourish and grow

Love is a two-way street where each spouse seeks to meet
both emotional and sexual needs
It is this type of spouse-to-spouse awareness, that helps to
quell outside passions and greed

Love is not a one-sided situation
Where we abandon our spouse in overloaded frustrations

Love is not a one-way street
Where only the physical or intimate needs, we meet

Love is not a one-sided deal
If one persists in one-sidedness, the enemy will surely steal

God is love and real love is of Him
He wants marriages to operate in His Love, not in
unpredictable or unsettling whims

Boundaries

Now that I'm married...
I can't go to some of the places I used to go
I can't seek the attention of others and want to be the show
Boundaries…

Now that I'm married...
I can't do some of the things I used to do
I can't live in selfishness, I have to think about you
Boundaries…

Now that I'm married...
I can't say some of the things I used to say
I can't be forward, I must speak a different way
Boundaries…

Now that I'm married...
I can't act some of the ways I used to act
Married life is a different walk, I must realize this fact
Boundaries…

Now that I'm married...
I can't stay on the phone for two or three hours at a time
I can't neglect my responsibilities, I must shift my
paradigm
Boundaries…

Now that I'm married...
I can't constantly be on social media minute by minute or
hour after hour

I can't spend most of my time there, because it might make my spouse sour
Boundaries…

Now that I'm married…
I can't talk to some of the people I used to talk to
I can't allow my good to be evil spoken of, I don't want to do anything to undermine you
Boundaries…

Now that I'm married…
I can't act as though I am still unmarried or single
I can't present myself flirty or available, when I socialize or mingle
Boundaries...

Now that I'm married…
I can't put everyone else first and my spouse last
I can't show dishonor, but to my vows I must hold fast
Boundaries…

Now that I'm married…
I can't put my spouse's needs on the back burner
I can't operate in ignorance, but I must be a swift learner or discerner
Boundaries…

Now that I'm married…
I can't have secret conversations, meetings, or meals with the opposite sex or my exes

I can't minimize or downplay such situations which can cause all kinds of messes
Boundaries...

Now that I'm married…
My life has changed and will change a great deal
I am humbled and willing to face what this life does reveal
So Dear God, I pray for your blessings, grace, and your holy seal.
Boundaries...

I Am Here for You

I am here for you
on the good days and on the bad

I am here for you
even the times that you are sad

I am here for you
You don't have to fear

I am here for you
I see your pain and tears

I am here for you
I will patiently wait for you to grow

I am here for you
I want to enjoy this moment and more

I am here for you
When you don't feel or act your best

I am here for you
On my shoulders, you can safely rest

I am here for you
I will be a friend in your midnight hour

I am here for you
I will constantly remind you of God's mighty power

I am here for you
When it's stormy and when it rains

I am here for you
I will walk with you through life's pain

I am here for you
not just physically, but emotionally

I am here for you
Not just emotionally, but day by day spiritually

I am here for you
I want our relationship to last

I am here for you
We must push forward and never dwell on the past

I am here for you
My commitment to our relationship is for life

I am here for you
By the grace and strength of the Lord Jesus Christ

Sex in Marriage

Sex in marriage is a beautiful thing
It is ordained and approved by the Eternal King

It is a union, a union like no other
It is a union and relationship that God will cover

The sacredness that happens between a man and woman
Is a heavenly seal and it's not uncommon

The interactions of the two are as natural as natural can be
God has ordained this union, Oh can't you see?

Sex is not to be approached with an uncaring attitude, or to be treated like a score
It is a holy, sacred coming together, so please don't make the Lord sore

The mixing of chemicals or body fluids are a part of God's plan
It is in this intimate union, He has chosen to reproduce man

Sex in marriage is naturally meant to be
It is where two become one unto Thee

It is a bond of oneness which delights the Lord
It is a bond of unity which the couple should look toward

It is a bond that should not be broken
It is a bond that represents a heavenly token

A token of commitment between just two
A vow, a sacred promise to each other to be true

Sex in marriage should not be used as a weapon
Remember God is on the throne, He is the witness from
Heaven

Neither should it be used as a deceitful or manipulative tool
To cause someone to feel used, taken advantage of, or
made a fool

Sex should be an understood and mutual agreement
It should never be abused or used as mistreatment

Sex in marriage is... a beautiful thing
It is indeed ordained and approved by our Heavenly King

When the Thrill is Gone

When the thrill is gone,
What will we do
Will we sit around staring into space
Or, will we look at the situation with a Boldface?

When the thrill is gone,
What will we do
Will we point the finger at each other
Or, will we sit down humbly and talk to one Another?

When the thrill is gone,
What will we do
Will we slip and slide into someone else's arms
Or, will we join hands and pray so that the devil won't
bring Harm?

When the thrill is gone,
What will we do
Will we grab hold to the word of God
Or, will we allow the enemy to kick up his Deceitful and
Lying Sod?

When the thrill is gone,
What will we do
Will we stir up the memories that we have held so dear
Or, will we relinquish what we have shared Year by Year?

When the thrill is gone,
What will we do

Will we reach deep inside ourselves to find the solution to the problem
Or, will we put our marriage in file 13, or in an "I Don't Care" column?

When the thrill is gone,
What will we do
Will we make a hasty or fleshly decision
Or, will we pray and wait for God's Divine Intervention?

When the thrill is gone,
What will we do
Will we bring a third party into the mix
Or, will we allow God to manifest a Heavenly Fix?

When the thrill is gone,
What will we do
Will we remain stuck in a rut or in a sense of dissatisfaction
Or, will we rise up in Faith and Take Some Action?

When the thrill is gone,
What will we do
Will we stay in bitter strife and in misery live
Or, will we humble ourselves and be Willing to Forgive?

When the thrill is gone... What will we do?

Love verses Lust

Love and Lust are two words with several similarities.
They both begin with the same letter which have the very same sound.
They both also have only four letters.
However, they are vastly different in their meanings!

Love denotes commitment, the determination to stick and stay
Lust denotes instability or uncertainty which can change day to day

Love says, "I am with you through thick and thin"
Lust says, "I am with you only if I Can win...win...win"

Love will stay with you through sickness and disease
Lust will bail out whenever it is not pleased

Love will stand for the things that are pure and right
Lust will fail or falter, and God's word it will slight

Love will be willing to acknowledge God and pray
Lust will look to self and do things its own way

Love will humble itself and say, "I am wrong"
Lust will self-exalt and deny God on the throne

Love will resist temptation and walk away from a flirt
Lust will throw caution to the wind and agree with the dirt

Love will consider the other person and how they might feel
Lust will be self-absorbed, not caring what it steals

Love will be there long after the money is gone or is low
Lust will be there as long as there is money, but after that, it has to Go!

Love will be there even when the fire starts to dwindle
Lust will do its own thing, don't have time for No Rekindle

Love will hold you tight, never want to let you go
Lust will drop you like a hot potato and show you to the door

Love and Lust are two words with several similarities
But don't fool yourself, they are vastly different in meaning!

Honest Eyes

The bible says that the eyes are the light of the body
It is our job to ensure they are not acting or behaving naughty

They reveal what the heart is secretly wanting, craving, or desiring
Therefore, planting God's word in the heart helps influence what they(the eyes) are admiring

Be careful where you place them, how you let them roam
They just might get you in trouble, you could be without a home

Eyes are for looking, but just don't look too long
For if you look too long, lust will give birth or motivate you to do the thing that is wrong

Know when to put them down, when to look away
This will help you avoid satan's snares, keep you from going astray

These glorious eyes that God has given can lead to mental or physical adultery
If they're not managed, your life can be filled with brokenness, heartbreak, and sexual idolatry

Don't put your eyes in the wrong place and think that it's okay

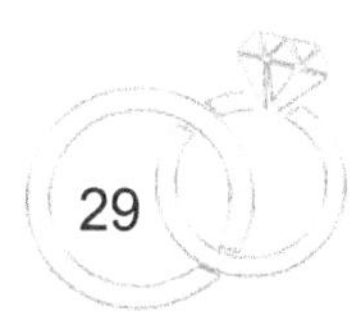

Remember God is looking, it is his desire that every part of you behave in a righteous way

Don't look a person up and down as though you're neglected or in need
This might kindle jealousy or anger in your spouse because of your repulsive lust or greed

Don't put your eyes on pornography and say, "Oh, I'm... just looking"
Do you not realize foolish man or woman just what the devil is cooking?

He's cooking and planning your demise, your very own desolation
While you are thinking you're okay, he's plotting your ultimate destruction!

Honest eyes are eyes that look, but not for the intention of lust
They are trained to look away, before the enemy can corrupt

Honest eyes are eyes that see the opposite sex only as a person
They don't reduce them to a body part, nor contemplate ungodly seduction

Honest eyes are eyes that see each person as God's divine creation

They refuse to undermine someone's worth with flirty, sexual solicitations.

Honest eyes are eyes that see every person as a human being
They don't allow the enemy to pervert or sexualize, the beauty of the person they're seeing

Honest eyes are managed by the purity of one's heart, the soul that has been soaked in the word of God and his Son's blood

The heart or soul that is cleansed in this manner will cause the eyes to see, Everyone as God's beloved

So by God's grace and power, keep your eyes in the right place for He has given you Everything you need

If indeed you choose to follow his word and integrity, your Marriage Will Surely Succeed!

Your Papa Was a Rolling Stone

Your Papa was a rolling stone...
But what does that have to do with you?
You have to decide if to yourself, you will be honest and true.

Your Papa was a rolling stone...
But do you have to repeat his lifestyle?
You have the freedom to choose, you don't have to be beguiled.

Your Papa was a rolling stone...
But do you have to walk in his insecurities?
You can walk in integrity and establish your very own stabilities.

Your Papa was a rolling stone...
But do you have to go from house to house?
You have a chance to stand up, be a man, and stop acting like a mouse.

Your Papa was a rolling stone...
But can you at least be honest and tell the truth?
You can take a stand now by putting away your childish and sinful youth.

Your Papa was a rolling stone...
But do you have to leave your children just like he did?

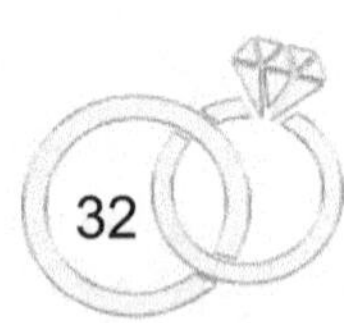

You have a chance to stand up and be a man, so stop acting like a kid!

Your Papa was a rolling stone...
But can you stop making insincere and broken vows?
You can be sincere and stop treating women like worthless objects, or using them like they're merely cash cows.

Your Papa was a rolling stone...
But do you have to be disrespectful to women or the opposite sex?
You could humble yourself, call upon God, allow him to clean up your mess.

Your Papa was a rolling stone...
But can you stop creating broken hearts and get a life?
You can be a faithful man, a husband to only one wife.

Your Papa was a rolling stone...
But do you have to turn to alcohol and drugs?
You can make a decision not to appear on any "police website or any wanted mug."

Your Papa was a rolling stone…
But do you know just how it really affected him?
You can make your own choices, or choose a life like his which was destructively grim.

Your Papa was a rolling stone...
But do you have to follow in his footsteps?

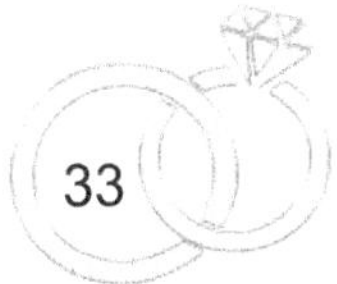

You can open your heart to God, and his Son you can accept.

Momma Stuck

Your Momma was a very important person in your life
She did many great things, but can't be exalted to the status of Christ.

She cradled you in her arms and showed you love
Now you must look to the Almighty God above.

She wiped your face and cleaned up all... your messes
But God will be with you through all your tests.

Your Momma took up for you, even when you were wrong
Time to look to God now, He's still on the throne.

I know you miss your Momma, and it's sad she's gone
Put your hands in God's hand, cause you got to go on!

She may have did some things that just wasn't right
Now on the living God, you must set your sights.

If she withheld information, she thought she was doing the right thing
Now you must pray it out, speak it out, to the King of kings.

She made mistakes in life because she wasn't perfect or without fault
You must decide whether you will forgive her or hold on to an ought.

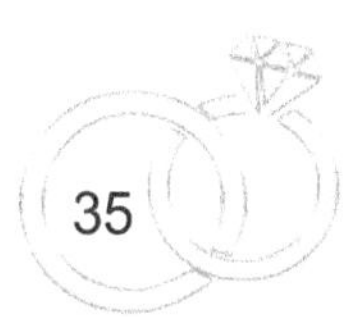

Your Momma had broken relationships, sometimes she was in the wrong
But don't get stuck there, you've got to write your own song.

Things happened to her that she just couldn't speak or utter
If you knew her whole story, it might make your heart break or flutter.

The intensity of anger or frustration that you occasionally witnessed
Doesn't have to be your fate if you choose the power of forgiveness.

The fear, hostility, and mistrust of men that she sometimes had
Doesn't have to dominate your life or make you sad or mad.

Your Momma wouldn't take any stuff off of people and certainly no man
She learned to be strong, self-sufficient, and for herself take a stand.

You must model your life after the positive examples that she both made and displayed
But be equally willing to relinquish, the non-positive things that leave you dismayed.

You must hold fast to the good things that she both said and did

Yet, let go of the things that cause you to be stuck, for God forbids.

Pray Together

Pray Together when times are prosperous and good
Humbly pray together like a devoted couple should

Pray Together in the times that there are misunderstandings
Humbly pray together when life seems so... demanding

Pray Together when you're not sure what to do
Humbly pray together and trust God to see you through

Pray Together when the enemy attacks your home
Humbly pray together, God will keep you in the zone

Pray Together when the enemy tries to pull you apart
Humbly pray together, God will put peace in your hearts

Pray Together when the enemy tries to pit you against each other
Humbly pray together, God will be your divine shield and cover

Pray Together in the times of sickness and disease
Humbly pray together, God will bring comfort and ease

Pray Together when times get rough and hard
Humbly pray together, God will be your strength and guard

Pray Together when you feel like you want to walk out the door

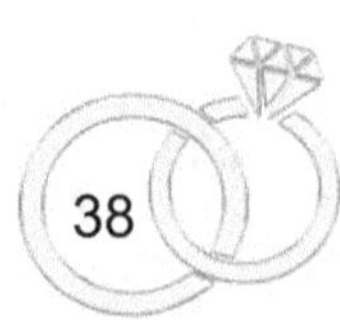

Humbly pray together, ask God for courage and
determination more and more

Pray Together when children are disrespectful and are
going astray
Humbly pray together, God will save them in his own time
and way

Pray Together when the enemy tries to destroy your life, or
turn your life upside down
Humbly pray together, stay in the word and on a strong
foundation you will be found

Pray Together when finances are low and friends are few
Humbly pray together, for God will fulfill his word and
give you friends that are fit for you!

Pray Together...Pray Together...Humbly Pray Together.

Take God as Your Partner

Honey, You don't have enough sugar to keep your
marriage sweet
Take God as your partner, He will help keep it orderly and
neat

Honey, You can't have enough sex to keep your marriage
in place
Take God as your partner, He will give you his keeping
grace

You may try to control or manipulate your spouse with
all... your sexy moves
Take God as your partner, trust that his word and power
still rules

Is your ego so... swollen, that you think you're as fine as
wine?
Take God as your partner, And, neither to thyself or to thy
beauty build a shrine

You may trust in the shape of your body to hold on to your
mate
Take God as your partner, Stop living in fantasy before it's
too late

Because gravity will shift the shape of your body one day,
what was Firm will turn to Sag
Take God as your partner, for when that happens, you will
have no room to brag

You may think of yourself as being so... buff, handsome, and irresistible
Take God as your partner, for he will give you a mindset that is so...sobering and biblical

You may try to intimidate with anger, control with fear
Take God as your partner, for he hears and sees Everything, because He Is Near!

When problems arise in your marriage as they surely will
Take God as your partner, trust that it will mend and heal

When you face storms in your marriage, don't know quite what to do
Take God as your partner, He will take care of you and see you through.

Always remember, the only third party in marriage should be the power of the Holy Ghost
Take God as your partner, for if He's not there, where is your boast?

The Bible says, a threefold cord (God, husband & wife) is not easily broken
Take God as your partner, stand on the infallible and holy word that He has spoken

Jesus Christ wants to be the author and finisher of your marital faith
Take Him as your partner, only on Him should your marital relationship be based.

The Perfect Mate

The perfect mate is someone who accepts you for who you are
On your lowest day, they purpose to make you feel like you're a star

The perfect mate is someone who shows respect to you and for you
They are determined to give you the honor and respect that is rightfully due

The perfect mate is someone who will stand up for you
They will stick with you, no matter what you go through

The perfect mate is someone who is exclusively committed to you
They understand your expectation of fidelity and have vowed to be true

The perfect mate is someone who is reliable and very trustworthy
They won't seek to undermine your worth by being an old jive turkey

The perfect mate is someone who helps to promote your dreams and purpose
Their support of you is not superficial or just on the surface

The perfect mate is someone who listens to you, chooses to hear your heart

They understand that listening is a way to quench or put out satan's fiery darts

The perfect mate is someone who will be honest, truthful with their spouse
They understand that honesty is key in the relationship, for it promotes peace in the house

The perfect mate is someone who doesn't mind being accountable of what they have done or where they have been
They take their marriage serious, not trying to risk it, by dibbling and dabbling in sin

The perfect mate is someone who shares in responsibility
They don't mind working with their hands to create marital and family stability

The perfect mate will make mistakes, and Honey, that's a given
Therefore, remember that by God's grace we have all been forgiven

The perfect mate will have flaws, and Honey, you do too
So before you judge him or her, look in your own mirror's view

The perfect mate will sometimes make the wrong decisions or choices
So please talk things over with God, before listening to all other voices

The perfect mate will sometimes get on your very, very last nerve
But be careful not to render to them, what you think they deserve

The perfect mate will sometimes get heated and operate in foolish pride
Trust and lean on God, for his word will not be denied!

The perfect mate is NOT perfect at ALL, but **IS** the person who is well suited for you and you for them

Therefore, both mates must perfectly work at the relationship, in order, to discover the hidden and precious marital gems

Crossing the Line

When you command or demand your spouse,
you are Crossing the Line.

When you call your spouse out of their name,
you are Crossing the Line.

When you curse or swear at your spouse,
you are Crossing the Line.

When you are verbally, mentally, or physically abusive,
you are Crossing the Line.

When you bring a third party into the marital relationship,
you are Crossing the Line.

When you put your marital sexual business in the streets,
you are Crossing the Line.

When you defraud your spouse sexually or in any manner,
you are Crossing the Line.

When you maximize your opinion while minimizing your
spouse's,
you are Crossing the Line.

When you exalt your needs and debase your spouse's,
you are Crossing the Line.

When you destructively criticize or debase your spouse privately or publicly,
you are Crossing the Line.

When you over compliment someone of the opposite sex,
you are Crossing the Line.

When you give time and attention that is due your spouse to someone else,
you are Crossing the Line.

When you allow someone else to have more power or influence in your life than your spouse,
you are Crossing the Line.

When you fail to defend or protect your spouse or relationship,
You Are Crossing the Line!

Submission verses Servitude

Godly submission is the willingness to yield to authority
It should not be forced thereby invoking fear or inferiority. (Servitude)

Godly submission is yielding to those in charge
It should not be pushy, intrusive, or angrily barged. (Servitude)

Godly submission should never strip one of their self-esteem
It should not be brute, over the top, or piercingly mean. (Servitude)

Godly submission should come out of a place of honor and true respect
It should not be rendered out of timidity or bitter disrespect. (Servitude)

Godly submission is deferring to others, putting others first
It should not be trampled upon, nor used to make one feel as though they're being cursed. (Servitude)

Godly submission should be based upon the holy, pure word of God
It should not be used to make one feel insignificant, taken advantage of, or as though, they are something odd. (Servitude)

Godly submission of the wife should be to the husband first

It should not be pretentious, insincere, neither should it be coerced. (Servitude)

Godly submission of the wife to the husband should pertain to the things that are right
It should not be to things that violates one's conscience, or that are forbidden (displeasing) in the Almighty God's sight (Servitude)

Godly submission is saying yes to any reasonable or godly requests
Yet, it should not be considered rebellion when one says No, and has scriptural basis upon which to rest. (Servitude)

Godly submission is being cooperative, agreeable with the person you have chosen
It should not be forced obedience or compliance that leaves the spouse's spirit damaged or broken. (Servitude)

Godly submission should be a mutual understanding from the word of God between the husband and wife
It should not be filled with one-sidedness, selfishness, or domination which will surely lead to chaotic strife (Servitude)

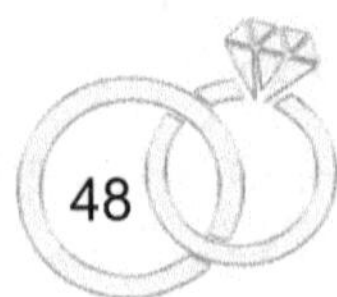

Headship Means Leadership Not Godship

The husband should lead the wife with wisdom, care, and love
He should realize that she has been given to him from the Heavenly Father above

The husband should lead by setting a righteous and godly example
He should be a bright light to his wife, like a burning luminous candle

The husband should humbly and clearly share the marital and family vision
He should lead in such a way that does not promote strife and division

The husband should be the spiritual leader that is noted for the word, prayer, and church fellowship
He should exemplify the qualities of true manhood and at all cost model godly leadership (headship)

The husband should lead with love, honor, and stability
He should live a life before his family that doesn't damage his credibility

The husband should be the protector, bear the ultimate responsibility for his spouse
He should be willing to take care of her, provide whatever is needed for their house.

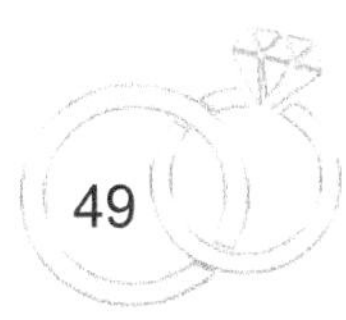

The husband has been given the oversight for his household, is not to dump it on his wife
This is a commandment from the Almighty God and the Lord Jesus Christ

The husband should not lead out of a spirit of domination and control
He should lead out of love and consideration, knowing God has given him this role

The husband should not lead out of tyranny or fear
He should lead out of godly humility, cherishing the one that is dear

The husband should not lead by attempting to force the wife into godly submission
He should lead by modeling the kind of man that convinces her of his marital and family vision

The husband should not lead by using physical abuse or constraint
He should lead realizing that he is her husband, But her God, he ain't!

The husband should not lead by attempting to browbeat the wife with the holy scriptures
He should lead by daily demonstrating that Christ is indeed his focus and his heavenly picture

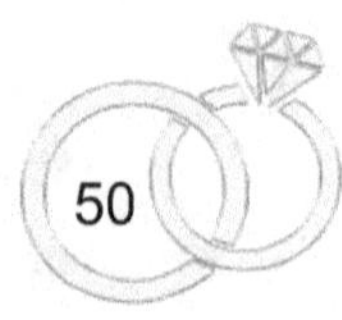

Please Forgive Me

Please forgive me when I hurt your feelings and walked away
When I didn't make things right between us that very day

Please forgive me when I gave you the silent treatment
When I shut you out, thereby rendering you mistreatment

Please forgive me when I lifted my voice and yelled at you
When I didn't consider what my tone and words would do

Please forgive me when I exalted someone over the person that you are
When I didn't realize how I undermined you and left a horrible scar

Please forgive me when I acted in pride instead of godly humility
When I didn't understand it would hurt our relationship and my credibility

Please forgive me when I took someone else's side against you
When I doubted and didn't bank on the person I knew-I knew

Please forgive me when I held your past over your head
When I brought it up again and again even though the issue was dead

Please forgive me when I've wanted you to be perfect and without flaw
When I failed to look at myself and use love as my law

Please forgive me when I was hasty with my words and sharp with my tongue
When I didn't respond in wisdom but to foolish pride I clung

Please forgive me when I didn't consider you, but it was all about I...I...I
When I didn't discern your inward needs nor your gentle cry

Please... Please, Forgive me

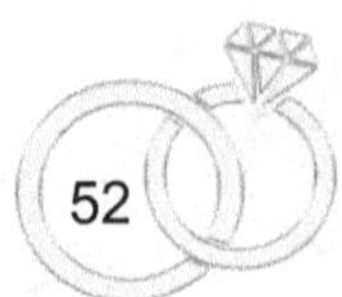

One King & One Queen for the Castle

One King & One Queen for the castle is quite all that we need
For if there is more...the enemy will have entrance and seek to deceive

One King & One Queen for the castle helps to keep loyalty intact
For if there is more...the marital foundation might well crack

One King & One Queen for the castle helps to minimize chaos and confusion
For if there is more...it might lead to an evil or deadly collusion

One King & One Queen for the castle helps to set necessary boundaries
For if there is more...it may lead to misunderstandings or create unwanted memories

One King & One Queen for the castle gives space for marital expectations to be established
For if there is more...the relationship's commitment might sever or even ultimately vanish

One King & One Queen for the castle helps to promote togetherness and growth
For if there is more...the enemy might take advantage, bring a breach between you both

One King & One Queen for the castle helps ensure that no third person has the final word
For if there is more... that third person might sway a spouse against what God has said

One King & One Queen for the castle helps to keep fidelity or faithfulness at the very forefront
For if there is more...one might be blind-sided by a friend whose motives are to have a secret, seductive hunt

One King & One Queen for the castle is a shield against everyone being in your personal business
For if there is more...a tattler or so-called friend might become your very own false witness

One King & One Queen for the castle gives an opportunity for two lives to be meshed together by the hand of God

For if there is more…The King & Queen might miss God's glory, and only be left with a fake or pretentious facade

The Seductive Dude

The seductive dude will try to get over any way he can
His life is built on nothing less than sinking grains of sand

The seductive dude is as slick as slick can be
His heart longs to deceive others, for that is all he can see

He is both rude in his motivations and in his actions
However, for some of the ladies, it is a daring attraction

He has a way with words, that is so very smooth
Be careful and alert that he doesn't make you his fool

The seductive dude thrives on "out thinking or out talking" his womanly prey
He loves to weave his web of deception to convince a woman to stay or lay

The seductive dude doesn't care about marriage nor about commitment
His only interest is in using, his manly and physical equipment

He constantly spills out lies upon lies
But the truth about his intentions, he strongly and firmly denies

He wakes early in the morning with a plan to execute his crafty con, secure his win

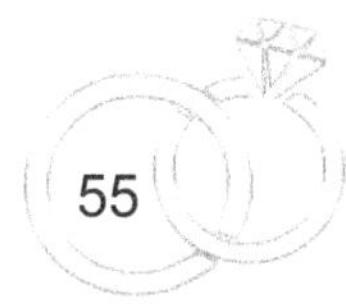

His ego is so swollen, eyes are so...blinded, that he doesn't see or care about the horrible cost of sin

The seductive dude might wear a fancy suit or just a pair of jeans
Whatever the case, please be aware that he's full of deceitful, deadly schemes

The seductive dude is sneaky, manipulative, and tries to control one's mind
In all actuality, he undermines true manhood, the glory that God has designed

A Man is Going to Be a Man

We have heard it said, “A Man is going to be a man,”
But does the scripture say, he can do anything he thinks he can?

“A Man is going to be a man,” implies that a man is going to be flirty, doggish, and unfaithful because this is the accepted and expected norm

But does the scripture bear witness to this mindset (way of thinking)
or must the man also be transformed?

“A Man is going to be a man,” also implies that even a married man is undoubtedly or inevitably going to cheat on his wife by having illicit affairs

But does not the scripture say, they are Both commanded to be faithful in order to avoid these types of snares?

“A Man is going to be a man,” suggests that fidelity or faithfulness is a hopeless cause or expectation
But does not the scripture say, God has made a way for everyone to escape every single temptation?

A Man is going to be a man,” also suggests that even God expects the man to fail
But doesn’t the scripture say, He wills for every Man to be saved and escape the woes (torments) of hell?

A real man practices self-control and walks in godly integrity
He allows God's spirit to bring conviction and constraint to avoid sexual infidelity

A real man realizes that his life doesn't consist of sex, sex, and more sex
He knows that he needs God's help to keep his whole body in check

A real man understands that his manhood is not based on how many women he deceives into bed
He has a confident awareness of himself and thoughtfully avoids the tears that could be shed

A real man is concerned about being able to honestly look into the face of his wife and child
He values their relationships, opinions, and flees from anything or anyone that seeks to beguile

A real man does not remain proud or haughty even when he makes a mistake
He humbly apologizes, prays to God, and asks if He will not allow his family to Break!

A real man walks away or flees from temptations and ungodly solicitations
He knows that such indulgence will end in humiliation, devastation, or even possible eternal damnation

A Woman is Going to Do Her Thing Too!

We have heard it said, “A Woman is going to do her thing too.”
But does the scripture say, she can do anything she chooses to do?

“A Woman is going to do her thing too,” implies that she has the right to match any misbehavior of her man
But does not the scripture say, we all have an appointment with God, before his judgment seat we shall stand?

“A Woman is going to do her thing too,” also implies that she has a mindset of stepping outside the marriage and doing her extra deeds

But does not the scripture say, God is not mocked, so one best be careful of sowing their treacherous seeds?

“A Woman is going to do her thing too,” suggests that she has thrown caution to the wind, put God’s word on the shelf

But does not God call his women to be virtuous, faithful, and honorable thereby showing respect for herself?

“A Woman is going to do her thing too,” also suggests that a woman is not chaste, pure, or sexually satisfied
But doesn’t the scripture say, All of our needs through God are absolutely and completely supplied?

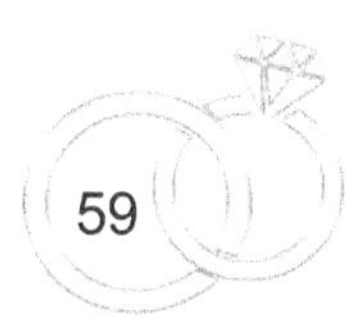

A real woman will work to walk in integrity, keep her name honorable and clean
She does not seek outside attention and desperately crave to be seen

A real woman carries herself with respect, dresses in modesty as to not draw outside attention
She does not carry herself provocatively as to stir up sexual appetites or contentions

A real woman wants to be able to look with pure eyes into the face of her husband and child
She carefully considers the consequences if she allows herself to be beguiled

A real woman humbles herself even if the husband has stepped out, done the wrong thing
She does not try to match his choice or out of rageful revenge have a sexual fling

A real woman humbles herself to pray when faced with both flirtations and temptations
She knows that if she yields to such, it will lead to humiliation, devastation, and possible eternal damnation

I'm Sorry

I'm Sorry are two powerful words that can change the course of life
When they are withheld, the relationship can be filled with unnecessary strife

I'm Sorry are two magical words that can change the mood of an entire atmosphere
When they are not uttered, the atmosphere can be filled with darkness, gloom, and fear

I'm Sorry are two important words that are filled with godly humility
When they are not spoken, the relationship lingers in state of disability or futility

I'm Sorry are two key words needed for any marriage to grow
When they are not expressed, the relationship can stop or move painfully slow

I'm Sorry are two critical words needed for one to be able to move from resentment to a place of forgiveness
When they are not released, the marriage suffers under the influences of pride, anger, and bitterness

I'm Sorry are two vital words needed to break the chains of harsh communication
When they are not sown or spoken, the enemy can continually work to bring further disconnection

I'm Sorry are two humbling words that can help stop separation and divorce
When they are not said, the enemy has space to work and his plan he will try to force

I'm Sorry are two crucial words that can save families from splitting up or going into separate directions
When they are not expressed, the marriage can become carried away by satan's lies and deceptions

I'm Sorry are two serious words that can melt away a stony heart
When they are not spoken, God has nothing to work with to give the marriage a restart

I'm Sorry are two powerful words that can push pride right out of the way
When they are withheld, God's hands are tied or restrained in convincing a spouse to stay

I'm Sorry...I'm Sorry...I humbly say, I'm Sorry

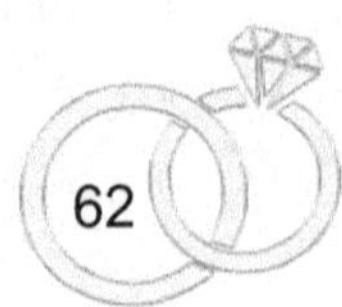

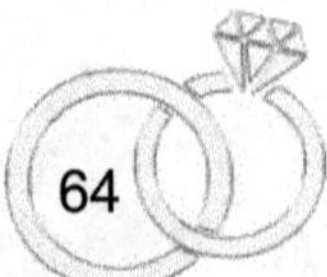

www.ingramcontent.com/pod-product-compliance
Lightning Source LLC
LaVergne TN
LVHW010542100826
845148LV00013B/2572